Money

CANDY 10¢

50¢

¢

$

BY SARA PISTOIA

Published by The Child's World®
1980 Lookout Drive • Mankato, MN 56003-1705
800-599-READ • www.childsworld.com

Acknowledgments
The Child's World®: Mary Berendes, Publishing Director
The Design Lab: Design
Editing: Jody Jensen Shaffer

Photographs ©: David M. Budd Photography

ISBN 9781623235321
LCCN 2013931354

Printed in the United States of America
Mankato, MN
July, 2013
PA02173

ABOUT THE AUTHOR

Sara Pistoia is a retired elementary teacher living in Southern California with her husband and a variety of pets. In authoring this series, she draws on the experience of many years of teaching first and second graders.

How do we use **money**?

We use money to **buy** things. We give other people money, and they give us something in return. Using money is a form of **trading**.

Long ago, people did not use money. When they needed something, they traded other items or their time.

Today people use money instead. They sell items or they sell their time, and they get money in return. Then they use the money to buy things.

Do you ever trade things with your friends? Then you know what trading is all about!

Counting is important when you use money. Have you seen these **coins**?

A **penny** = one **cent**

A **nickel** = five cents

A **dime** = ten cents

A **quarter** = twenty-five cents

Can you count these pennies?

Each penny is **worth** one cent.

You need to count by ones.

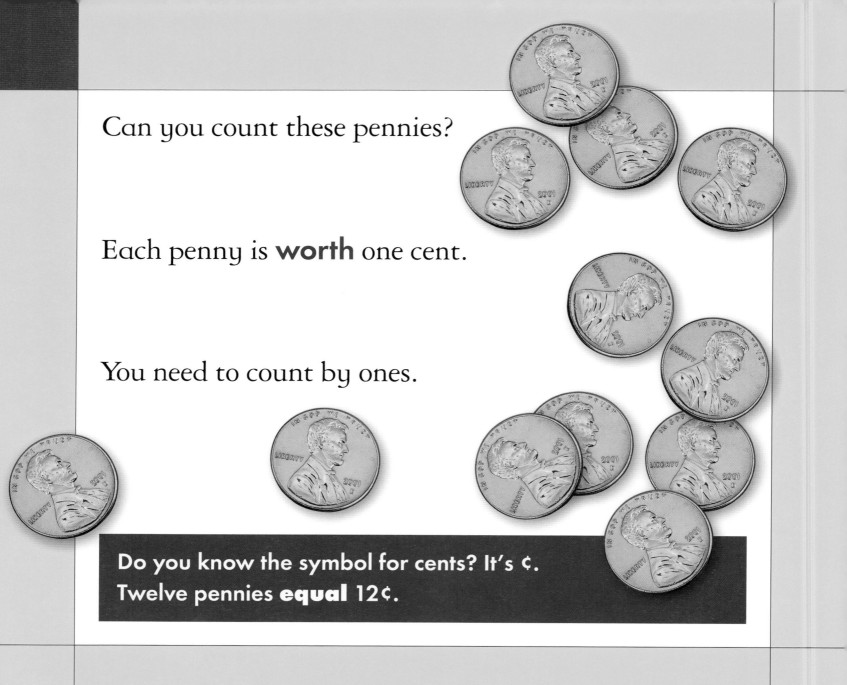

Do you know the symbol for cents? It's ¢.
Twelve pennies **equal** 12¢.

1¢   2¢   3¢   4¢   5¢

6¢   7¢   8¢   9¢   10¢

11¢   12¢

Did you count to twelve? That means you have twelve cents.

Here are some nickels.
Each nickel is worth
five cents.

Can you tell how much these nickels are worth?

You need to count by fives.

5¢   10¢   15¢   20¢   25¢

Did you count twenty-five cents?

13

A dime is worth ten cents. With dimes, you count by tens to add them together.

Try adding these dimes together, counting by tens.

| 10¢ | 20¢ | 30¢ | 40¢ |

| 50¢ | 60¢ | 70¢ | 80¢ |

Wow! You have eighty cents!

This candy costs ten cents.

Do you have enough money to buy it?

When you have mixed coins to count, start with the highest **value**. A nickel is worth more than a penny, so it has a higher value.

How much are one nickel and five pennies worth?
Are they the same as one dime?

Count to find out!

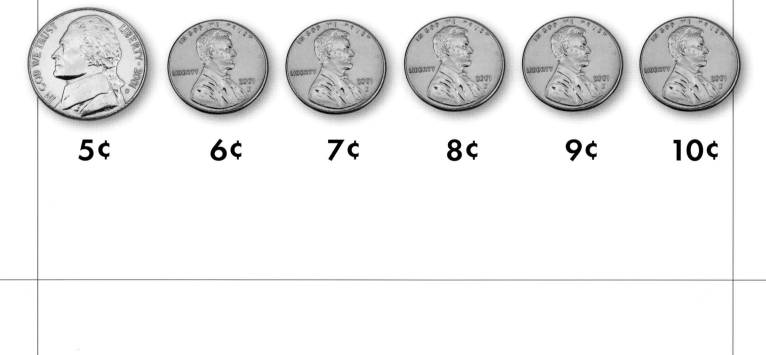

5¢   6¢   7¢   8¢   9¢   10¢

If you have one quarter, you have twenty-five cents. You could trade your quarter for other coins. What coins could you get?

Five nickels equal one quarter.

5¢   5¢   5¢

5¢   5¢   =   25¢

Two dimes and one nickel equal a quarter.

Count them and see!

10¢   10¢   5¢   =   25¢

Do you have enough money to buy this toy bear?

Start counting with the coin that is worth the most.

Finish with the coin that is worth the least.

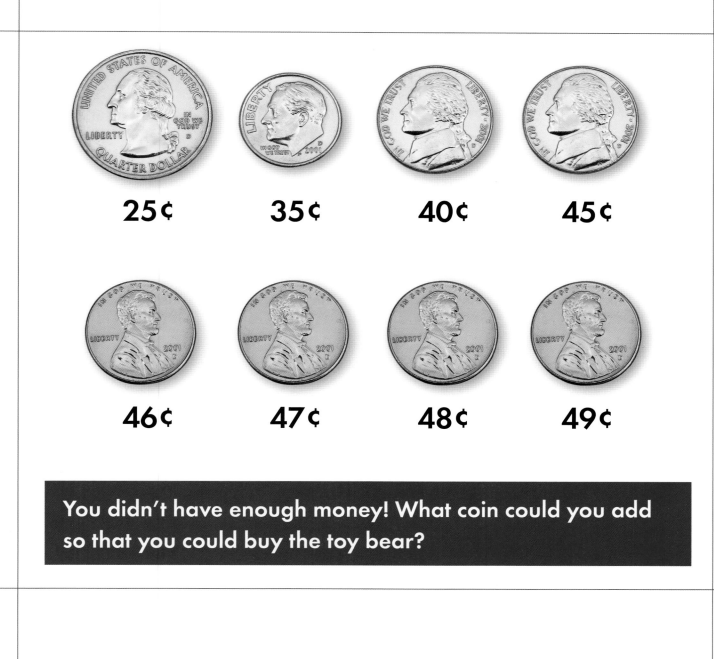

25¢   35¢   40¢   45¢

46¢   47¢   48¢   49¢

You didn't have enough money! What coin could you add so that you could buy the toy bear?

Do you **earn** money for helping at home?

Count the coins you have earned by doing chores.

25¢   **35¢**   **45¢**   **50¢**

You might want to save your money so you don't spend it right away. Piggy banks are a great place to keep your money safe!

Money is part of
our lives.

You can spend money
and you can save
money.

It's important to know
how to count money!

Key Words

buy

cent

coins

dime

earn

equal

money

nickel

penny

quarter

trading

value

worth

Index